Mel Bay's
Beginning
MANDOLIN SOLOS

by William Bay & Frank Zucco

CD CONTENTS
Performed by Dix Bruce

1 Tune Up [:59]	16 Red Oak [:25]	31 Over the Waves [:55]	46 Old Folks at Home [1:04]
2 Big Mama Polka [:45]	17 Sally Goodun [:33]	32 Invitation to the Dance [:49]	47 American Patrol [1:30]
3 She'll Be Coming Around the Mountain [:40]	18 Cape Cod Girls [:33]	33 Can Can [:46]	48 Blue Danube Waltz & Du Du [1:40]
4 Aura Lee [1:03]	19 The Cowboy [:49]	34 The Caissons Go Rolling Along [:54]	49 Miss McCloud's Reel [:44]
5 Away Rio [:35]	20 Chicken in the Hayloft [1:16]	35 Come to the Sea [:58]	50 Nearer My God to Thee [1:05]
6 Di Di Dum [:58]	21 Cowboy Jack [:47]	36 Minuet [:39]	51 Sarah-Ann Waltz [1:03]
7 Yellow Rose of Texas [:41]	22 My Gal on the Rio Grande [:32]	37 Something for the Pick [2:37]	52 Hole in Her Stocking [1:06]
8 Red River Valley [:58]	23 Mama's Gone [:57]	38 O' Susanna [:46]	53 Frank's Tune [:36]
9 Under the Double Eagle [:48]	24 Sourwood Mountain [:28]	39 Come Back to Torrino [:46]	54 Sugar in the Gourd [1:02]
10 Cripple Creek [:36]	25 My Home's Across the Smoky Mountains [:44]	40 Dark Eyes [:54]	55 Sailor's Hornpipe [:37]
11 Ol' Dan Tucker [:36]	26 Wildwood Flower [:42]	41 Caprice [1:08]	56 Fiddler's Break [:25]
12 Crawdad Song [:33]	27 Liberty [:37]	42 Santa Lucia [1:09]	57 Pizzicato Polka and Le Secret [1:23]
13 Ol' Joe Clark [:34]	28 Arkansas P.Q. [:47]	43 Waves of the Danube [1:24]	
14 John Henry [:30]	29 Hatikvoh [:44]	44 Turkish March [1:44]	
15 Careless Love [:50]	30 Gypsy Dance [:46]	45 Country Gardens [:44]	

1 2 3 4 5 6 7 8 9 0

Visit us on the Web at http://www.melbay.com — E-mail us at email@melbay.com

Contents

How To Read Tablature
(Diagrams)
The Mandolin Fingerboard

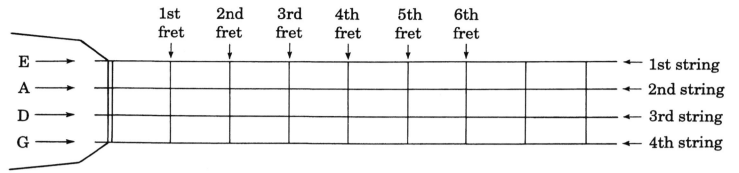

The mandolin consists of eight strings divided into four pairs and each pair is tuned in unison. In tablature, we use only one line to represent both strings.

Tablature

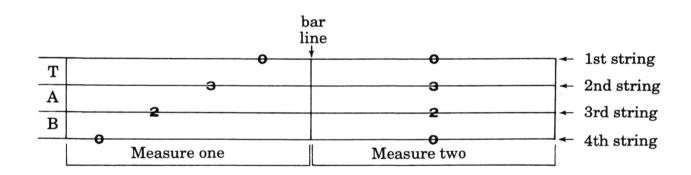

Tablature (TAB) is simply a drawing of four lines to represent the strings with numbers, to show either picking the strings open or in which fret to press strings down to produce the note called for in music. When two or more notes are played at the same time the numbers are above one another. In the 1st measure of the example above play as follows:

4th string is played open
3rd string is played on the 2nd fret
2nd string is played on the 3rd fret
1st string is played open

In the 2nd measure, the same notes are shown as a chord and should be played at the same time.

Big Mama Polka

She'll Be Coming Around The Mountain

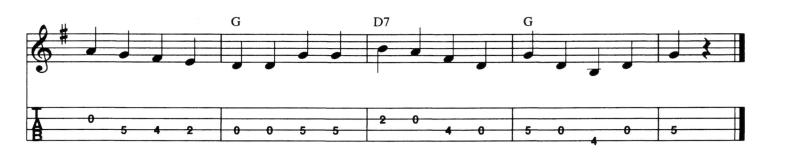

Aura Lee

TRADITIONAL

Away Rio

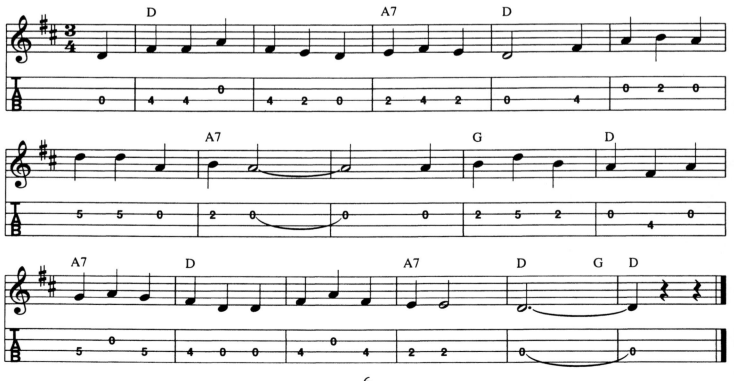

Di Di Dum
(Written especially for Mandolin)

FRANK ZUCCO

Yellow Rose Of Texas

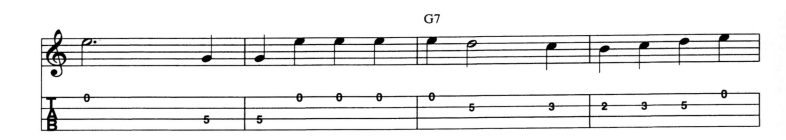

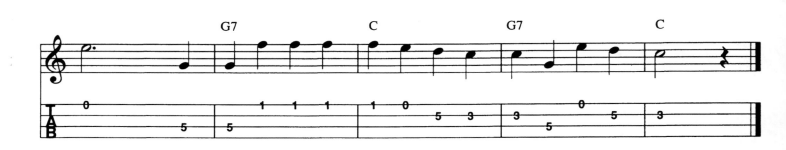

Red River Valley

Under The Double Eagle

Cripple Creek

Ol' Dan Tucker

Crawdad Song

Old Joe Clark

John Henry

Careless Love

Red Oak

F. Zucco

Sally Goodun

Cape Cod Girls

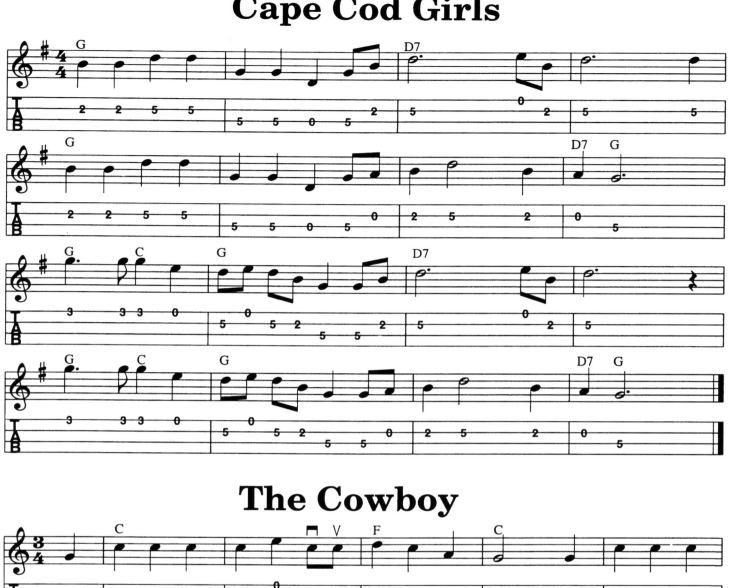

The Cowboy

Chicken In The Hayloft

F. Zucco

Cowboy Jack

My Gal On The Rio Grande

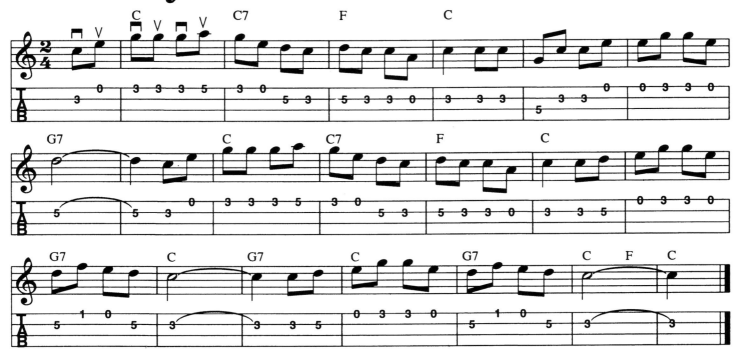

Mama's Gone

F. C. Z.

Sourwood Mountain

My Home's Across The Smoky Mountain

Wildwood Flower

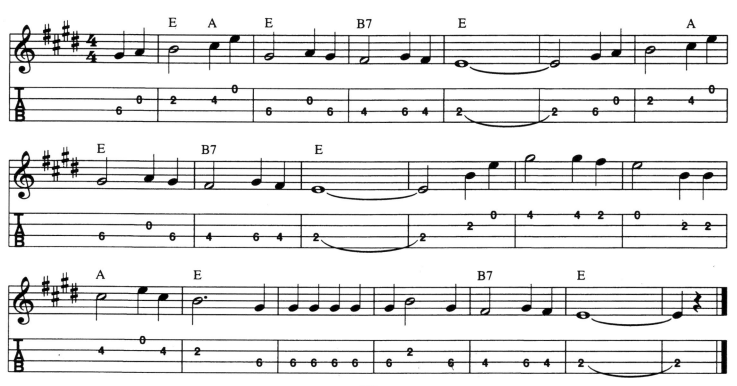

Liberty

Arkansas P. Q.

F. Zucco

Hatikvoh

Gypsy Dance

V. HERBERT

Over The Waves

ROSAS

Invitation To The Dance

C. M. VON WEBER

Can Can

The Caissons Go Rolling Along

Come To The Sea

Minuet

BACH

Something For The Pick

O' Susannna

Come Back To Torrino

F. C. Z.

Dark Eyes

GYPSY SONG

Caprice

N. PAGANINI

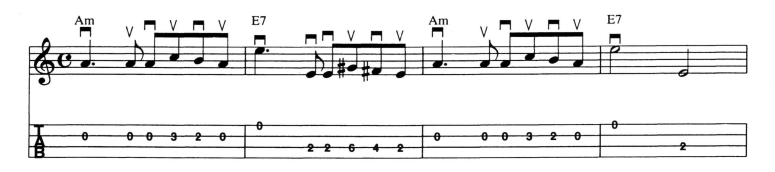

Santa Lucia

Waves Of The Danube

IVANAVICI

Turkish March

BEETHOVEN

Country Gardens

Old Folks At Home

FOSTER

American Patrol

MEACHAM

Blue Danube Waltz & Du Du

J. STRAUSS

Miss McCloud's Reel

Nearer My God To Thee

L. MASON

Sarah-Ann Waltz

F. C. Z.

Hole In Her Stocking

Frank's Tune

F. C. Z.

Sugar In The Gourd

Sailor's Hornpipe

Fiddler's Break

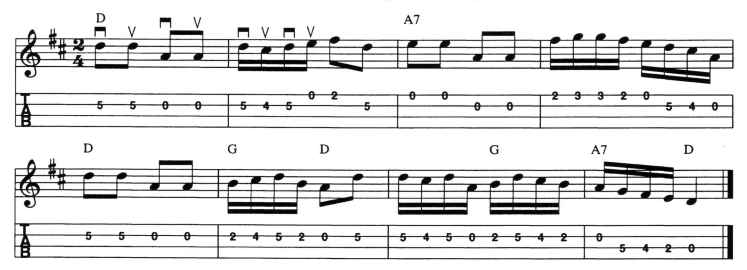

Pizzicato Polka and Le Secret

DELIBES & GAUTIER